NATIONAL GEOGRAPHIC KIDS™

HALLOWEEN BOOK OF FUN!

NATIONAL GEOGRAPHIC

WASHINGTON, D.C.

The National Geographic Society is one of the world's largest nonprofit
scientific and educational organizations. Founded in 1888 to "increase
and diffuse geographic knowledge," the Society works to inspire people to
care about the planet. National Geographic reflects the world through its
magazines, television programs, films, music and radio, books, DVDs, maps,
exhibitions, live events, school publishing programs, interactive media and
merchandise. *National Geographic* magazine, the Society's official journal,
published in English and 33 local-language editions, is read by more than
38 million people each month. The National Geographic Channel reaches
320 million households in 34 languages in 166 countries. National Geographic
Digital Media receives more than 15 million visitors a month. National
Geographic has funded more than 9,400 scientific research, conservation
and exploration projects and supports an education program promoting
geography literacy.

For more information, visit nationalgeographic.com,
call 1-800-NGS LINE (647-5463), or
write to the following address:
National Geographic Society
1145 17th Street N.W.
Washington, D.C. 20036-4688 U.S.A.

Visit us online at www.nationalgeographic.com/books

For librarians and teachers: www.ngchildrensbooks.org

More for kids from National Geographic: kids.nationalgeographic.com

For information about special discounts for bulk purchases, please contact
National Geographic Books Special Sales: ngspecsales@ngs.org

For rights or permissions inquiries, please contact National Geographic Books
Subsidiary Rights: ngbookrights@ngs.org

ISBN: 978-1-4263-0848-2

Printed in China
11/RRDS/1

Halloween, Games, Jokes, Crafts, and More!

p. 28

D are to enter this frightfully fun book and you'll find 80 pages packed with Halloween games, jokes, crafts, pumpkin carving tips, and more. You'll find your way through a shadowy pumpkin patch, explore a haunted house, check out a Halloween pet parade, and fill in the blanks to your own ghost story.

Inside you'll find fun hidden pictures, photo games, optical illusions, matching games, and more, all with a spooky Halloween twist. More than 50 clever ideas for pumpkin carving, Halloween parties, and do-it-yourself costumes will make your home the scariest one the block this Halloween. Plus, you'll laugh at ghoulishly funny jokes and comics, and discover creepy weird-but-true trivia.

p. 33

Halloween Book of Fun! is the second book in the popular National Geographic Kids Book of Fun series. Pulled from the pages of NATIONAL GEOGRAPHIC KIDS magazine, these games and crafts are loved by kids everywhere. And because it comes from National Geographic, you'll learn about animals and fascinating facts, even as you play.

Game answers are at the back of the book, but try to figure them out on your own before you look. And be sure to ask a parent for help and permission before you make the crafts in this book. Most of all, remember to share the fun, and you're sure to have a "spooktacular" Halloween!

p. 40

Table of Contents

p. 19

p. 10

p. 41

p. 34

p. 38

4

p. 26

SPOOKY MYTHS BUSTED

p. 11

BET YOU DIDN'T KNOW

p. 13

DO-IT-YOURSELF

p. 54

MORE TRIVIA AND FUN!

ANSWERS

p. 21

CRAZY Costumes

It's the day before Halloween, and this costume shop is a mess! Kids are trying on costumes, but certain pieces are lost somewhere in the store. Find the missing costume parts listed below, then draw a line connecting each part to the correct costume.

* bat symbol from Batman's chest
* Darth Vader's light saber
* pirate's hook
* pumpkin's stem
* Harry Potter's glasses
* witch's broomstick
* vampire's fangs
* princess's tiara
* bunny's tail
* cat's ears

ANSWERS ON PAGE 77

What in the World?

HALLOWEEN HUES

These photographs show close-up and faraway views of orange and black objects. Unscramble the letters to identify what's in each picture.

ANSWERS ON PAGE 77

Play interactive "What in the World?" and other games online. kids.nationalgeographic.com

NAESK

RTRCAO

OGL REFI

MUTANU FALE

AKBCL TRAPHEN

TROSAICP

NTD'O LWKA NSGI

YOPPP DIFLE

INNPEUG

FUNNY FILL-IN

Spooked!

Ask a friend to give you words to fill in the blanks in this story without showing it to him or her. Then read out loud for a laugh.

IS THERE ANYONE OUT THERE?

On Halloween night I heard a(n) _____ knock at the front door. But my friends weren't
                                    adjective

supposed to show up for _____ more minutes to go trick-or-treating. "Is there anyone out
                          number

there?" I asked into the darkness. No one answered. Suddenly all the _____ turned
                                                                        household object, plural

off at once. A(n) _____ ran down my spine as I _____ toward the closet and
                    noun   *past-tense verb*

_____ hunted for a flashlight. But all I found was a(n) _____ and
  adverb ending in -ly   *electronic gadget*

last year's _____ beach towel. Just then the light from the _____
              cartoon character   *something in space*

shone through the window. I saw a wicked _____ and a(n) _____ animal
                                            fairy tale creature   *adjective*

outside, _____ toward me! "_____!" I screamed. Then I heard
           verb ending in -ing   *fairy tale creature*

_____ laughing like a(n) _____ . That's when I realized that
  male family member's name   *animal*

the scary creature was just a mask and cape that he had attached to a(n) _____ .
                                                                           object used for cleaning

And the animal? That was our pet _____ . Looks like I got a trick instead of a treat.
                                    different animal

MONSTER MAZE

START

CANDY APPLES

FINISH

Find your way through this haunted cornfield without getting spooked. Then circle ten witch's brooms hidden in the maze.

ANSWERS ON PAGE 77

SPELLBOUND

This wacky wizard is trying to make ten different animals magically appear. But he keeps creating objects that rhyme with the animals' names instead. For example, number one is a balloon rather than a baboon. Can you figure out which animals he meant to create? **Bonus: Do other animal names rhyme with any of these objects?**

ANSWERS ON PAGE 77

Back Talk

I'll hold him down while you guys tickle him.

What do YOU think this lemur is thinking? Fill in your own funny quote.

Spooky Myth Busted

SUPERSTITION

Knocking on wood keeps away misfortune.

WHERE IT CAME FROM

People used to believe that gods lived inside trees. If you knocked on wood when you wanted a favor, the tree gods would help you out.

WHY IT'S NONSENSE

You know supernatural beings don't live inside wood. But tree-loving critters might have fooled folks into thinking they did, says Linda Butler, who studies insects at West Virginia University. "Lots of noisy insects live inside trees," she says. "For instance, the larva of the pine sawyer beetle makes a loud gnawing sound when it chews on wood."

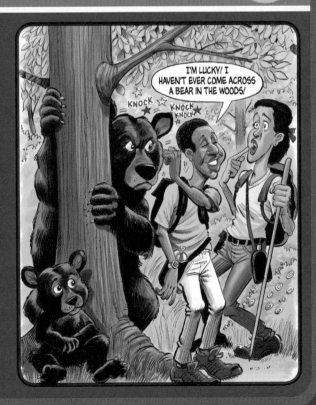

Hidden Halloween

Aunt Bertha's house is stranger than usual on Halloween. Find and circle the 15 hidden objects listed at right. ANSWERS ON PAGE 77

- lemon
- brain
- baseball
- bowling ball
- dollar bill
- bowling pin
- pocket comb
- piece of toast
- ice-cream cone
- cookie
- pizza slice
- steak
- pencil
- teacup
- fish

Trick or Treat

Bet you didn't know

⑦ Halloween FACTS to howl about

1 **Vampire bats** don't actually **suck blood**—they lap it up with their **tongues.**

2 More than **35 million pounds** of **candy corn** is produced each year in the U.S.— that's the **weight of 101 jumbo jets.**

3 **Pumpkins** and **witches** are the **most popular** Halloween costumes for **pets.**

4 The word **pumpkin** comes from the ancient Greek word *pepon,* meaning "ripe melon."

5 Competitors **race coffins** down the **main street** of a **Colorado town** every October.

6 Nearly half of Americans say they **believe in ghosts,** according to a CBS News poll.

7 **Diners eat** surrounded by **22** occupied **graves** at **a restaurant** in **India.**

Cool Costumes

SPAGHETTI & MEATBALLS

YOU WILL NEED
• LARGE CARDBOARD BOX • SMALL TABLECLOTH
• CRAFT GLUE • LARGE PLASTIC PLATE • CREAM-COLORED
YARN • BROWN POM-POMS • RED FELT • BASEBALL CAP
• PAPER NAPKIN • PLASTIC UTENSILS • PLASTIC SALT
AND PEPPER SHAKERS • PLASTIC VASE WITH FLOWERS

WHAT TO DO
Cut out a two-foot-wide circular piece of cardboard.
Cut holes in the center of the cardboard and
tablecloth for your head. Glue the tablecloth
to the cardboard. Cut a hole for your neck
out of the plate. Slit the plate so you can
wear it as a collar. Glue yarn (spaghetti),
pom-poms (meatballs), and red felt
(sauce) to the plate and cap.
Glue napkin, utensils, salt
and pepper shakers,
and a vase with
flowers on top of
the tablecloth.

CAT UP A TREE

YOU WILL NEED
• GREEN SHIRT • BROWN
PANTS • LEAFY GARLANDS
(AVAILABLE AT CRAFT STORES)
• SAFETY PINS • STUFFED
CAT • BOBBY PINS
OR ELASTIC
HEADBAND

WHAT TO DO
Wrap the garlands
around your arms
and torso, and
pin in place. Pin the
cat to your shoulder.
Attach leaves to your
hair with bobby pins or
by pinning them to a
headband. Your friends
will be green with envy.

14

BAT

YOU WILL NEED
- LARGE BLACK TRASH BAG • BLACK SHIRT AND PANTS • SAFETY PINS • THICK BLACK FELT • BOBBY PINS OR HEADBAND

WHAT TO DO
Cut the trash bag into two matching wing shapes. After you get dressed, ask an adult to safety pin the wings in place. Cut two triangle-shaped ears out of felt. Use bobby pins to hold them in place, or pin the ears to an elastic headband. Then swoop next door for some candy.

AQUARIUM

YOU WILL NEED
- LARGE CARDBOARD BOX
- SILVER PAINT OR CONSTRUCTION PAPER • BLUE CELLOPHANE • DUCT TAPE • CRAFT FOAM • FISHING LINE
- SEASHELLS • PLASTIC GREENERY (AVAILABLE AT CRAFT STORES)
- OPTIONAL: SNORKEL MASK OR GOGGLES AND FLIPPERS

WHAT TO DO
Cut a hole for your head in the top of the box. Cut large squares out of all four sides. Paint the box or cover it with construction paper. Cover the back window with a large piece of cellophane and tape it to the inside of the box. Tape strips of cellophane inside both side windows. Cut sea animal shapes out of craft foam. To hang, thread fishing line through a small hole in each shape, then tape the fishing line to the top of the box. Tie or tape fishing line around the seashells to hang them. Tape greenery inside the front of the box. If you like, wear a snorkel mask, goggles, or flippers for photos. For safety, be sure to remove them before you go trick-or-treating.

Do-It-Yourself

CHEESE & CRACKERS

YOU WILL NEED
- LARGE CARDBOARD BOX • YELLOW PAINT
- EMPTY BOX OF CRACKERS

WHAT TO DO
Cut off the bottom of a large, narrow, rectangular box. Then cut off the narrow sides stopping about four inches from the top. Now cut the front and back of the box into V-shapes. To create the Swiss cheese effect, cut several holes in both sides. Finally, cut a hole in the top of the box for your head. Apply a few coats of yellow paint. Wear an empty cracker box as a hat.

SHARK

YOU WILL NEED
- WHITE POSTER BOARD
- TAPE • GRAY HOODED SWEATSHIRT •GRAY FOAM SHEET OR CARD-BOARD PAINTED GRAY
- SAFETY PINS

WHAT TO DO
Cut triangles from white poster board and tape them inside the hood of a gray sweatshirt. Cut a fin shape from a gray foam sheet (available at craft stores). In the center of the fin's base cut a one-inch vertical slit. Fold one side out to the right and the other side out to the left. Secure each side to the back of the sweat-shirt using safety pins.

YOU WILL NEED

• LARGE CARDBOARD BOX • CLEAR PACKING TAPE • RED AND WHITE CONSTRUCTION PAPER • GLUE • POPPED, UNBUTTERED POPCORN • MARKER • BASEBALL CAP

WHAT TO DO

Cut off the bottom of the box for your legs and cut circles in the top and sides for your head and arms. Tape the seams of the box. Glue strips of colored paper to all four sides. Make a "POPCORN" sign and attach it to the front. Glue popcorn to the top of the box and baseball cap. Your costume will be so "pop-ular"!

CLOTHES DRYER

YOU WILL NEED

• LARGE CARDBOARD BOX
• PAPER PACKING TAPE
• WHITE PAINT • BRUSH
• JAR LIDS • EMPTY BOX OF DRYER SHEETS

WHAT TO DO

Cut the bottom off of a large square cardboard box. Cut holes in the box for your head and arms. Cut a door in the front of the box. (Cut along three sides, then fold open slightly.) To create the control panel, take some of the excess cardboard, fold it, and place crease side up along the back edge of the box. Tape into place. Brush on several coats of white paint. Use white jar lids to make the dials. Tape on an empty box of dryer sheets for decoration.

Do-It-Yourself

LAUNDRY

YOU WILL NEED
• PLASTIC LAUNDRY BASKET
• HEAVY STRING • PACKING
TAPE • COLORFUL CLOTHES

WHAT TO DO
Cut a hole the width of your body in the bottom of a thin plastic laundry basket. (The opening needs to be big enough so you can slide the basket over your shoulders to your waist.) Loop heavy string through the slats in the sides of the basket and tie it around your waist. Put strips of tape across the hole in the bottom so clothes won't fall out. Fill the basket with colorful clothes.

JELLY BEANS

YOU WILL NEED
• LARGE CLEAR PLASTIC BAG • COLORED BALLOONS
• RED FELT MARKER
• STRIP OF WHITE POSTER BOARD • RIBBON
• BLACK SWEAT SUIT

WHAT TO DO
Make holes for your arms and legs in the bottom and sides of a large, clear plastic bag. (A lawn bag or a dry-cleaner bag works well.) Put the bag on over your clothes, then fill with different colored balloons. Gather the bag opening at your neck and loosely tie on a tag made with the poster board and red marker.

SPIDER

YOU WILL NEED
• BLACK TIGHTS • RED FELT • BLACK YARN
• BLACK SHIRT AND PANTS
• STYROFOAM BALLS (OR SOCKS) • SAFETY PINS

WHAT TO DO
To create the legs, take three pairs of inexpensive black tights and fill each leg with styrofoam balls (available at craft stores) or rolled-up pairs of socks. Tie black yarn between the first and second balls that you put into each spider leg. Leave enough yarn to tie around your wrists so you can raise and lower the legs. Pin or sew the open ends of the tights to the back of a black shirt and wear black pants. To be a black widow spider, cut an hourglass shape from red felt or fabric and pin it to the front of the shirt. To make a skullcap, cut one of the feet off a pair of black tights or stockings.

SHOWER

YOU WILL NEED
• SMALL HULA HOOP • SHOWER CURTAIN AND RINGS • CLEAR PACKING TAPE • CARDBOARD TUBE• METALLIC CONSTRUCTION PAPER • SILVER TINSEL • SHOWER CAP • BACK BRUSH

WHAT TO DO
Use the shower curtain rings to hang the curtain from the hula hoop. Stretch tape across the hula hoop, creating straps to rest on your shoulders. Wrap metallic paper around the cardboard tube to make the shower pipe. Form a cone shape out of metallic paper to create the showerhead. Tape it to the top of the shower pipe and tape tinsel to the inside of the spout so it looks like spraying water. Securely attach the pipe to the hula hoop with tape. Your costume will make quite a splash!

LION

YOU WILL NEED
• YELLOW HOODED SWEAT SUIT • YELLOW FELT • THICK, FUZZY YELLOW AND BROWN YARN • SAFETY PINS • FACE PAINT

WHAT TO DO
For the lion's mane, cut a piece of yarn long enough to tie around your face with the hood up. Tie three-inch-long pieces of yellow and brown yarn all along the string. Make furry cuffs for your wrists the same way. For the tail, cut a long strip of felt and glue yarn to the end. Cut two ears out of the felt. Tie the lion's mane around your hood and secure it with safety pins. Pin the ears and tail in place and tie on the fur cuffs. Paint on a brown nose and whiskers, and practice your roar.

FAKE BLOOD

You will need
- measuring spoons
- small bowl
- plastic spoon
- 3 tablespoons maple syrup
- 15 drops red food coloring
- 1 drop green food coloring

WARNING: Food coloring stains clothes, so dress for a mess!

Directions
Mix the maple syrup and food coloring. Dribble it on your skin and/or lips. (It tastes yummy!)

Removal Tip: If you are still slightly "blood-stained" after using soap and water, scrub skin with an astringent pad.

SCARY SCABS

You will need
- microwave-safe bowl
- 1 cup cold water
- 1 packet unflavored gelatin
- light corn syrup
- cornmeal
- 2 small paintbrushes
- dark red lipstick

Directions

1. Mix water and gelatin together in the bowl. Let the mixture stand for two minutes. Microwave on high for 40 seconds, then let stand for two more minutes until the gelatin has dissolved.

2. Place the mixture in the refrigerator until it cools (about 30 minutes).

3. Slather a thick layer of corn syrup onto your skin in the shape you want the scab to be.

4. Sprinkle a thick layer of cornmeal over the corn syrup. Let it sit for two minutes.

5. Gently tap off the excess cornmeal.

6. Use a paintbrush to gently dab lipstick onto the cornmeal. (Don't press too hard, or the cornmeal will crumble off.)

7. Use the second paintbrush to gently cover the cornmeal with a thin coating of gelatin.

8. After about 15 minutes, the gelatin will dry, sealing the scab.

HAIRY MOLES

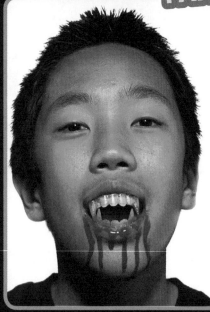

You will need
- 1 whole black peppercorn per mole
- eyelash glue
- bristles from a small paintbrush (about 3 per mole)

WARNING: Do not put moles near eyes. (The pepper will sting them.)

Directions

1. Put a dab of eyelash glue on your skin.

2. Place peppercorn on glue spot and hold until glue dries.

3. Dip one end of a bristle in glue and stick it to peppercorn. Repeat for hairier moles.

ASK FOR YOUR PARENTS' PERMISSION BEFORE YOU START AND FOR THEIR HELP IN GATHERING ALL THE THINGS YOU'LL NEED.

What Your HALLOWEEN COSTUME Says About You

There may be more to your Halloween costume than just looking good. "What you choose to be for Halloween may reflect your personality," says psychologist John Suler of Rider University in New Jersey. So, what are *you* going to be this year?

WITCH

Witch means "wise one" in an ancient language. Legend has it that witches traveled by broomstick and cast spells to stop bad guys. IF YOU'RE A WITCH, YOU...are always on the go, constantly flying from one activity to another. You use your smarts to help friends.

CLOWN

Clowns have entertained people for thousands of years. Modern clowns take their time—up to an hour—to apply their special makeup. IF YOU'RE A CLOWN, YOU...love entertaining friends with your sense of humor. You also take your time tackling big projects or decisions.

GHOST

Believers think most ghosts are shy. People claim they often see ghosts by themselves; the spirits rarely speak. IF YOU'RE A GHOST, YOU...are quiet, shy, and like to hang solo or with a few friends. Independent, you don't need much help from others.

PRINCESS

Princesses are known for their beauty, elegant clothes, and sparkling jewels. This costume is always a popular choice at Halloween. IF YOU'RE A PRINCESS, YOU...have a sparkling personality that makes you very popular. You take pride in your appearance and love to shop.

PIRATE

Pirates traditionally traveled by water in large groups. Loud and boisterous, they liked to have fun when they weren't looting ships. IF YOU'RE A PIRATE, YOU...are adventurous, always ready to have a good time with your friends. You love traveling and being outside.

CAT

Known for their curiosity and independence, cats like to explore and play. Cats enjoy their downtime, too, sleeping about 16 hours a day. IF YOU'RE A CAT, YOU...are fun-loving and like to check out cool new places. But when it's time to rest, you're ready to sleep late.

Find the ANIMALS in DISGUISE

Animals don't get dressed up for Halloween, but they do wear disguises to blend into their environments. Find the animals listed below in the pictures. Write the correct letters in the spaces provided. ANSWERS ON PAGE 77

1. jaguar _____
2. fish _____
3. arctic fox _____
4. shrimp _____
5. caterpillar _____
6. seahorse _____
7. crab _____
8. sea snake _____
9. katydid _____
10. moth _____
11. chameleon _____

B SCOTLAND

D SPAIN

E ITALY

A INDONESIA

C NORTHERN IRELAND

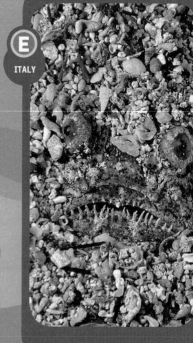

F COSTA RICA

I INDONESIA

G BRAZIL

J JAPAN

H CANADA

K INDONESIA

23

A Boo-tiful Halloween

Find at least ten items in the scene that rhyme with the word "boo." For example, the witch is stirring a "brew."
ANSWERS ON PAGE 77

Just Joking

KNOCK,
KNOCK.

Who's there?
Dewey.
Dewey who?
**Dewey have to
wait much longer
to eat?**

▶ **Bare-backed
fruit bat**

Q Where is a monster's
favorite place to swim?

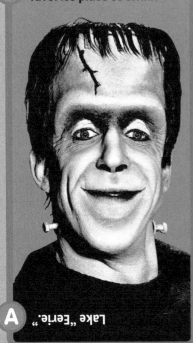

A Lake "Eerie."

**TONGUE
TWISTER!**

Say this fast three times:

6 silly
sisters
sort short socks.

Q How do
you fix a
broken
jack-o'-
lantern?

A With a pumpkin patch.

You've **got** to be joking...

Q What do you get if you
cross **Bambi** with a **ghost?**

A Bamboo.

25

You look like you've seen a ghost

What do YOU think this dog is thinking? Fill in your own funny quote.

Spooky Myth Busted

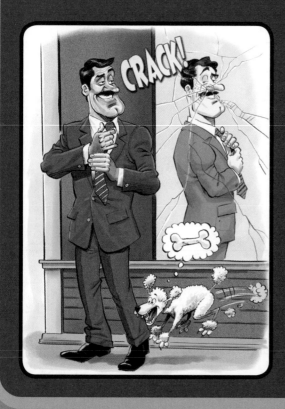

CRACK!

SUPERSTITION

Breaking a mirror means trouble.

WHERE IT CAME FROM

People used to believe that your reflection was actually your soul. So if you broke a mirror, you'd break—and therefore lose—your soul.

WHY IT'S NONSENSE

That's not your soul in the mirror—that's light! "When you look at any object in a mirror, what you're actually seeing is reflected light," says Lou Bloomfield, author of *How Things Work: The Physics of Everyday Life*. When you stand in front of a mirror, reflected light from your body bounces off the mirror's surface. That's why you see your reflection.

6 crazy facts
about
creepy crawlies

1

One of the world's **fastest snakes**— the black mamba— slithers up to **seven miles an hour.**

2

The **longest worms** can grow to at least a **hundred feet.**

4

More **beetles live on Earth** than any other **creature.**

3

The largest known **ant supercolony** stretches nearly **4,000 miles** through Portugal, Spain, France, and Italy.

5

Scorpions
glow under **black light.**

6

A male African cicada can make a sound as loud as a **power mower.**

Do-It-Yourself SPOOKY

FREAK OUT YOUR FRIENDS AT THE **COOLEST HALLOWEEN PARTY ON THE BLOCK.**

Ask for a parent's help and permission before you start these projects.

EYEBALL DEVILED EGGS

YOU WILL NEED
• 6 HARD-BOILED EGGS • 1/4 CUP MAYONNAISE • 1 TEASPOON MUSTARD • PINCH OF SALT • GREEN AND RED FOOD COLORING • SLICED BLACK OLIVES • TOOTHPICKS

WHAT TO DO
Peel the cooled eggs and slice them in half the long way. Scoop out the yolks into a bowl and mash them up. Mix in the mayonnaise, mustard, and salt. Stir in a few drops of green food coloring. Spoon the mixture into the center of the egg halves. Place a slice of olive on top of each half. Dip a toothpick into red food coloring, and then use it to draw lines on the eggs as shown. Now your eggs look like creepy eyeballs.

WACKY PUMPKIN

WHAT TO DO
Sketch a face on your pumpkin. Poke toothpicks into the pumpkin, and then use them to secure the vegetables. Use broccoli and lettuce for hair, cucumbers and cherry tomatoes for eyes, cauliflower for ears, a mushroom for the nose, and bell peppers and carrots for the mouth and teeth. Or create your own veggie vision.

HALLOWEEN PARTY!

SPECIMEN JARS

WHAT TO DO
Place plastic snakes, insects, eyeballs, hands, or even a fake brain inside jars with lids. Fill each jar with water and add drops of food coloring until you like how it looks. Add a few drops of milk to make the water cloudy, or experiment with mixing colors. The more disgusting-looking, the better!

WEREWOLF CUPCAKES

YOU WILL NEED
• CHOCOLATE CAKE MIX • INGREDIENTS ON CAKE MIX BOX •
2 CANS OF CHOCOLATE FROSTING • RED M&M's •
BLACK JELLY BEANS • RED GUMDROPS • CANDY CORN

WHAT TO DO
1. Make cupcakes according to the recipe on the box. Cool completely.

2. Place a large scoop of frosting on each cupcake. Spread a layer of frosting over the cupcake, but leave a big dollop in the center. Working from the outside in, stick the prongs of a fork into the top layer of frosting and gently pull it out to create a furlike texture. Repeat until the frosting is textured and evenly distributed.

3. Use M&M's for eyes, a jelly bean for the nose, a flattened gumdrop for the tongue, and the white part of candy corn for fangs. For a pointy nose, place a gumdrop under the icing in the center and half a jelly bean flat on top.

PUMPKIN CUPCAKES

YOU WILL NEED

- 1 CUP VEGETABLE OIL
- 3 CUPS SUGAR
- 4 EGGS
- 2 TEASPOONS VANILLA
- 4 CUPS FLOUR
- 4 TEASPOONS BAKING POWDER
- 1/2 TEASPOON SALT
- 2 TEASPOONS CINNAMON
- 1/2 TEASPOON NUTMEG
- 1/2 TEASPOON GINGER
- 1/4 TEASPOON GROUND CLOVES
- 2 CUPS CANNED PUMPKIN
- 16-OUNCE CONTAINER OF CREAM CHEESE FROSTING
- RED AND YELLOW FOOD COLORING (OPTIONAL)

WHAT TO DO

CUPCAKES: Preheat the oven to 350°F. Line two 12-cup muffin tins with baking cups. In one bowl, mix the oil, sugar, eggs, and vanilla extract. In a separate bowl, combine the remaining dry ingredients. Stir the wet ingredients into the dry ingredients just until blended. Add the pumpkin to the mixture. Distribute the batter evenly among the baking cups. Bake for 20 minutes. Cool completely before frosting.

ORANGE FROSTING (optional): Mix 24 drops of yellow food coloring and 8 drops of red into the frosting for a festive topping.

BIRD'S NEST SNACK MIX

YOU WILL NEED
- TOASTED PUMPKIN SEEDS
- RAISINS
- PRETZEL STICKS
- CHOCOLATE-COVERED PEANUT CANDIES
- CANDY CORN

WHAT TO DO
Mix all of the ingredients together in any amount that you like. Set out bowls of the mix for guests to snack on.

TRICK or TREATS for Dogs and Cats

DOG TREATS

YOU WILL NEED
- 1 CUP PEANUT BUTTER
- 1 CUP MILK
- 1 TABLESPOON MOLASSES
- 2 CUPS WHOLE WHEAT FLOUR
- 1 TABLESPOON BAKING POWDER
- COOKIE CUTTERS

WHAT TO DO
Preheat oven to 375°F. Mix the peanut butter, milk, and molasses. In a separate bowl, combine the flour and baking powder, then add it to the wet ingredients. Knead until blended and press into a ball. Roll out the dough on a lightly floured surface. Cut out shapes with the cookie cutters. Bake on a greased cookie sheet for 20 minutes. Cool before feeding to Fido.

REMEMBER THAT PETS SHOULD EAT TREATS IN MODERATION.

CAT TREATS

YOU WILL NEED
- 3 TABLESPOONS EGG WHITES, SCRAMBLED
- 6-OUNCE CAN OF TUNA PACKED IN WATER
- 1/4 CUP CORNMEAL
- 1/2 CUP WHOLE WHEAT FLOUR

WHAT TO DO
Preheat oven to 350°F. Chop up the scrambled egg whites and mix with all the other ingredients, including the water from the tuna. Press into a ball, then flatten the dough onto a greased cookie sheet. Cut the dough into bite-size pieces for cats. Bake for 20 minutes. Cool slightly. Kitty will like these served warm.

MORE FUN PARTY IDEAS

* Decorate with glow-in-the-dark paint and black-light bulbs.
* Paint monster footsteps leading to your front door.
* Make worm punch. Place gummy worms on the edge of the punch bowl.
* Hang wet strings over the doorway. Walking through the strings feels like sticky cobwebs.

MAKE A
Creepy
LAVA LAMP

HOW DOES IT WORK?

The secret behind the lamp's "lava" is science. Oil is lighter, or less dense, than water, so it rises to the surface. Salt is heavier, or more dense, than water and sinks to the bottom. When you add the salt, blobs of oil attach to the grains and sink. Then the salt dissolves and the oil returns to the top. The result? A liquid show for the eyes.

YOU WILL NEED

- clear jar with lid
- water
- food coloring
- glitter
- vegetable oil
- salt
- flashlight

WHAT TO DO

1. Fill the jar three-quarters full of water.
2. Add drops of food coloring until you like the color you see. A few drops go a long way! Sprinkle in glitter for extra sparkle.
3. Fill the jar almost to the top with vegetable oil and let the mixture separate.
4. Pour salt into the jar until you see the cool lava lamp effect. When the bubbles stop, add more salt to see it again.
5. Shine a flashlight behind the jar to watch your lava lamp really glow!

Back Talk

This is one dead party!

What do YOU think this skeleton is thinking? Fill in your own funny quote.

Spooky Myth Busted

SUPERSTITION   Ravens predict death.

WHERE IT CAME FROM

Ravens are scavengers, so they were often spotted at cemeteries and battlefields—places associated with dying. People started thinking the birds could predict death.

WHY IT'S NONSENSE

People who spot ravens could be in for some *good* luck—not death. Vikings sailing the ocean would release captive ravens and follow them toward land. If the birds returned, the sailors knew land was still far away. And tame ravens are very friendly. "They act like puppies," says Patricia Cole of New York City's Prospect Park Zoo. "They'll sit on your lap, let you scratch their heads, and play tug-of-war!"

Funny FILL-IN

Create Your Own Ghost Story!

Before you read this story, circle one of the orange words or phrases in each group of three below. Then read out loud for a laugh.

On Halloween night I dressed up as a princess | Spider-Man | Po the panda and decided to do jumping jacks | go trick-or-treating | turn cartwheels in the creepy | forbidden | gooey graveyard at the end of my street. Everyone says it's haunted | made of licorice | smelly, but I wanted to find out for myself. My dog Buster | Jelly Bean | Tinkles and I arrived after sunset, just as the night air was turning cold | minty-fresh | bright purple. I started to skip | count sheep | sing karaoke to keep the raccoons | ghosts | tooth fairy away, but it didn't work. Suddenly a baby-soft | freezing cold | bony hand scratched | tickled | pinched my toe | shoulder | nose. I jumped | backflipped | bounced at least 10 | 5,000 | a million feet in the air. But I didn't see anything behind me except for a gravestone | spiderweb | grilled-cheese sandwich. I figured it was just my mind | dog | goldfish playing tricks on me, so I kept walking. Then I heard footsteps | meows | bacon frying in the distance, and the sound was getting closer and closer. Just when I thought I might faint | eat breakfast | hug my teddy bear, my best friend jumped out from behind a gravestone and shouted "Boo!" | "Gotcha!" | "Happy Halloween!" I felt my face turn pale | bright red | green. I probably looked as if I really had seen a ghost | Darth Vader | the school principal.

Just Joking

Leaf-tailed gecko

KNOCK, KNOCK.

Who's there?
Phillip.
Phillip who?
Phillip my bag with treats, please!

Q What type of dogs do **vampires** like the best?

A Bloodhounds.

TONGUE TWISTER!

Say this fast three times:

Dracula digs dreary, dark dungeons.

Q What happens when a ghost gets lost in the fog?

A He is mist.

You've **got** to be joking...

Q What do you call **two spiders** that just got **married?**

A Newlywebs.

35

Haunted Room

This kid was surprised to find at least 14 Halloween-related objects scattered around his room. Find and circle them. ANSWERS ON PAGE 78

MUMMY AUTOPSY

R.I.P.

EYES

BRAIN

SLIGHTLY RUNNY SCRAMBLED EGGS

A CANNED WHOLE TOMATO

HEART

PEELED GRAPES

GUTS

FINGERNAILS

COOKED CURLY EGG NOODLES IN COOKING OIL

SLICED ALMONDS

PEANUTS

TOES

Your friends will be completely grossed out when they reach inside this creepy coffin. Gruesome foods inside feel like decaying body parts!

YOU WILL NEED

TALL MOVING BOX • PAINT (WHITE AND BLACK) • PAINT-BRUSHES • GLUE WASH (EQUAL PARTS WHITE GLUE AND WATER) • TOILET PAPER • MOSS (OPTIONAL) • COLORFUL PAPER • BLACK TRASH BAGS • SHOE BOXES

WHAT TO DO

1. First ask for a parent's help cutting the box. Cut a coffin shape out of the front panel of the box and outline a mummy shape on it. Paint the mummy white and the background black. When dry, cut out circles where the body parts will go.

2. Starting at the top, use a clean paintbrush to apply the glue wash to a small area. Stick on pieces of toilet paper, pinching the paper slightly for a wrinkled effect. Crisscross some pieces of paper to create a wrapped look. When you reach a hole, pull the paper through and glue it to the back. Repeat until the mummy is covered. Glue pieces of moss to the mummy if you like. Glue on paper labels for the body parts. Feeling creative? Make a coffin lid out of the back panel of the moving box.

3. Place the coffin on a table with shoe boxes under the holes to hold the bowls of food. Tape black trash bags to the underside of the cardboard and drape the bags over the sides of the table.

HALLOWEEN PET PARADE

You *expect* to see vampires, pirates, and witches on Halloween. What you don't expect is for those creatures to have four legs! Dressing up pets for Halloween is a huge trend. In fact, one survey found that one in ten dog owners put their four-legged friends in Halloween costumes. Check out these hilarious pet costumes.

Wonder if he went to Hogwarts? Toby the poodle casts a spell as a wizard.

Instead of candy, which can be bad for dogs and cats, treat your pet to Halloween snacks made just for them. Check out the recipes on page 31, or visit your local pet store.

Gretel the basset hound is dressed as former First Lady Jackie Kennedy.

Cha-Cha the miniature schnauzer is born to be wild dressed as a biker.

PLAYBILL

THE DOG KING

Who *wouldn't* follow Taz the Yorkshire terrier to the theater when he's dressed as a playbill?

Shayna the wheaten terrier is one cool cat—uh, *dog*—in her 1950s-style poodle skirt.

He "vants" to suck your blood! G.W. the miniature dachshund masquerades as a vampire.

Ferocious lion? Maybe not. But Chili the Boston terrier is still having a good hair day.

These pets like wearing costumes, but your pet may not. Never force your pet to do something it does not want to do.

Good dog! Looks like Boston the long-haired dachshund has wisely held the onions from his costume.

It's a bat! It's a dog! It's Emmy the miniature schnauzer as Batdog!

Maybe Duque the cocker spaniel can audition for the next *Pirates* movie!

Funny FILL-IN
Field of Screams

Ask a friend to give you words to fill in the blanks in this story without showing it to him or her. Then read out loud for a laugh.

On a dark and _____ (adjective) night, my friends and I decided to go on a(n) _____ (adjective) hayride. As we rode through the farmer's _____ (type of food) field, I felt a(n) _____ (noun) run down my spine. My friends laughed and playfully called me a scaredy- _____ (animal) . That's when we heard loud _____ (verb ending in -ing) all around us. " _____ (Exclamation) !" I yelled. My friends said it was probably just the wind _____ (verb ending in -ing) through the trees, but they were as pale as _____ (plural noun) . Suddenly, we saw the shape of a(n) _____ (adjective) monster appear out of thin _____ (noun) . It had _____ (color) skin and _____ (large number) arms, and it smelled like a rotten _____ (noun) . I screamed _____ (adverb) and _____ (past-tense verb) off the hay wagon. I wanted to get home as fast as my _____ (body part, plural) would carry me. My friends were right behind me. To this day we still have no idea what kind of _____ (adjective) creature we saw, but we won't be going back anytime soon to find out.

What in the World?

Play interactive "What in the World?" and other games online. kids.nationalgeographic.com

CREEPY CREATURES

These photographs show close-up views of creatures that slither and crawl. Unscramble the letters to identify what's in each picture.

ANSWERS ON PAGE 78

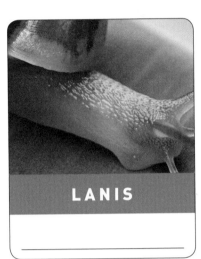

LANIS

_____

DEPISR

_____

ELETEB

_____

ESA GUSL

_____

KACCRHOOC

_____

RALTECILARP

_____

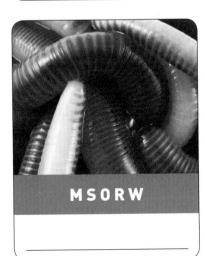

MSORW

_____

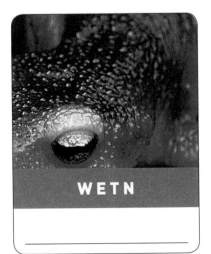

WETN

_____

LMEO

_____

Back Talk

I'm melting, I'm melting!

What do YOU think this witch is thinking? Fill in your own funny quote.

Spooky Myth Busted

SUPERSTITION

Awful stuff happens on Friday the 13th.

WHERE IT CAME FROM

According to Norse legend, a party thrown by 12 gods was spoiled by a murderous 13th god—making 13 an unlucky number. And Fridays were special to the Norse goddess Freya, so if you offended her on that day, watch out!

WHY IT'S NONSENSE

Many cultures believe that 13 is a *good* number. For instance, some Chinese people believe the number is lucky because it sounds like a phrase meaning "must be alive." And even though many buildings don't have a 13th floor (the elevator numbers go from floor 12 to floor 14), technically that's impossible. "The 14th floor *is* the 13th floor," says Joe McInerney, American Hotel and Lodging Association president. "And those floors never have any more problems than the other floors."

FRIDAY THE 13TH
PRESIDENT DECLARES FRIDAY THE 13TH NATIONAL HOLIDAY

Photo Find

Crazy Cornucopia

Oops! Someone knocked over a fall cornucopia. Find and circle these items:

turtle	4 crayons
seashell	penny
bug	6 pinecones
key	cherry
8 bananas	monkey
deer	3 footballs
airplane	duck
2 umbrellas	cookie cutter

ANSWERS ON PAGE 78

Just Joking

KNOCK, KNOCK.

Who's there?
Boo.
Boo who?
Don't cry. I'm just a trick-or-treater!

▶ Aye-Aye

ANOTHER LAME JOKE

Q Why didn't the skeleton dance at the party?

A He had no body to dance with.

TONGUE TWISTER!

Say this fast three times:

Which witch watched which witch walk?

Q What did Dracula say about his girlfriend?

A It was love at first bite.

You've **got** to be joking...

Q What are a **monster's** two **favorite** states?

A North and South Scarolina.

44

Funny FILL-IN
Fright Night

Ask a friend to give you words to fill in the blanks in this hair-raising tale without showing it to him or her. Then read it out loud for a laugh.

_____ woke up with a jolt of fear. There was something at the foot of his bed.
male movie star

It was _____. It smelled of _____. He couldn't see more than a (an)
adjective   snack food

_____-shaped shadowy figure, but its breath sounded like a (an) _____.
type of fruit   type of transportation

_____ pulled his _____ sheets up over his _____ as he
same male movie star   cartoon character   body part

_____ up the courage to _____. "What do you want?" he asked in a (an)
verb ending in -ed   animal sound

_____ voice. The _____ figure hissed its reply. "I...want...all...your..._____!"
adjective   adjective   your favorite candy

_____ yanked the covers off his _____. There stood _____, his
same male movie star   body part   female name

_____ sister. "I want them NOW!" she _____. "You took all of the
adjective   noisy verb ending in -ed

_____ out of my trick-or-treat bag. So hand over the _____ or I'm going
plural noun   your favorite candy

to tell _____, and you'll have to _____ the
family member   present-tense verb

_____ for a whole _____!"
animal   time period

Visual Tricks or Treats

Do you see a young woman or an old lady?

Tilt the page back to find out what these are.

Which skeleton is tallest?

ANSWER ON PAGE 78

45

Do-It-Yourself

PUMPKIN CARVING

A PUMPKIN ARTIST SHARES HIS AMAZING CARVING SECRETS.

What do Harry Potter and Scooby-Doo have in common? Their faces have been carved on jack-o'-lanterns! Known as the Picasso of pumpkin carving, artist Hugh McMahon slices and dices the gourds to make them look like celebrity faces, crazy masks, and wild animals. NG KIDS got the inside goop, er, scoop on carving like a pro.

HUGH McMAHON CARVES A 930-POUND PUMPKIN.

NGK: WHAT'S IT LIKE TO BE UP TO YOUR ELBOWS IN ORANGE GOO?
McMAHON: Messy! Sometimes I slip on seeds and pumpkin gunk. And a 150-pound, barrel-size pumpkin once fell on my toe.

NGK: OUCH! WAS THAT THE HEAVIEST PUMPKIN YOU'VE CARVED?
McMAHON: Nope. Some have weighed 1,000 pounds! One Thanksgiving I carved a turkey shape in a three-foot-wide pumpkin for the White House, but it wouldn't fit through the x-ray machine at security. The police dogs just sniffed at the pumpkin. Finally the guards waved me through.

NGK: WHAT'S YOUR JACK-O'-LANTERN CARVING SECRET?
McMAHON: I make them glow brighter by peeling off the skin in places and letting the inside flesh show through.

NGK: WHAT'S THE HARDEST THING ABOUT WORKING WITH PUMPKINS?
McMAHON: Mice love to eat them. Sometimes I come to work and my pumpkins have been nibbled.

A pumpkin is a fruit, not a vegetable.

OCTOPUS

ZEBRAS

Some Native Americans use pumpkin seeds in medicines.

CAT WITCH

TIPS AND TRICKS

SCOOBY-DOO

MUMMY

HARRY POTTER

ORANGUTAN

Jack-o'-lanterns originated hundreds of years ago in Scotland and Ireland. Locals placed lit-up turnips outside their homes to scare away evil spirits.

When the Scots and Irish immigrated to the United States, they switched to pumpkins.

CARVE PERFECT PUMPKINS!

Create awesome jack-o'-lanterns with these tips from artist Hugh McMahon.

1 Pick a pumpkin that's shaped similar to the head of the character you want to carve.

2 Slice off the bottom of your pumpkin instead of the top to hide the knife line. Then scoop out the seeds.

3 Draw a design on the pumpkin with a water-based marker. Cut along the lines.

4 The more teeth you carve, the scarier your jack-o'-lantern will look.

5 Spray carved pumpkins with lemon juice to prevent wrinkles; soak shriveled pumpkins in water for a quick face-lift.

USE A CHILD-SAFE KNIFE, OR ASK YOUR PARENTS FOR HELP BEFORE CARVING.

Do-It-Yourself

You don't have to be a professional to carve amazing pumpkins. Use these tips to make cool pumpkins like these at home.

STACK ATTACK
BUILD A SKELETON OR SNOWMAN BY STACKING THREE PUMPKINS. SLANT THE KNIFE WHEN YOU CUT OFF EACH STEM, CREATING A SHELF FOR ANOTHER PUMPKIN.

CAST A SPELL
CARVE HALLOWEEN MESSAGES ON YOUR PUMPKINS. PLACE THEM NEAR THE FRONT DOOR TO WELCOME— OR SPOOK—TRICK- OR-TREATERS.

THE NOSE KNOWS
WHO SAYS STEMS HAVE TO BE ON TOP? TURN A CURVY STEM INTO A FUNNY NOSE.

COSTUME PARTY USE SNORKEL GEAR, SILLY HATS, INEXPENSIVE JEWELRY, AND OTHER ACCESSORIES TO MAKE CLEVER COSTUMES FOR YOUR PUMPKINS.

MAKE A SCENE ARRANGE YOUR JACK-O'-LANTERNS SO THEY'RE "REACTING" TO EACH OTHER.

FACE-TO-FACE SKIP THE CARVING KNIFE AND PAINT FUNNY FACES ON YOUR PUMPKINS INSTEAD.

SHOOT FOR THE STARS CARVE PLANETS, FLOWERS, FISH, SPIDERS, OR ANYTHING ELSE YOU LIKE.

BOLD AND *BOO*-TIFUL PAINT PUMPKINS WHITE FOR A GHOSTLY EFFECT.

LIGHT SHOW THIS PTERODACTYL WAS CREATED BY AN ARTIST, BUT YOU CAN GIVE ANY PUMPKIN THIS UNUSUAL GLOW.

TRACE A DESIGN ON THE PUMPKIN. THEN PEEL OFF THE OUTER SKIN IN A FEW PLACES, LEAVING THE FLESH UNDERNEATH INTACT. PLACE A LIGHT INSIDE AND ADMIRE YOUR WORK.

Back Talk

Why are you in such a good mood?

What do YOU think this cat is thinking? Fill in your own funny quote.

SUPERSTITION

Throwing salt over your left shoulder wards off evil.

WHERE IT CAME FROM

Salt was very valuable because it preserved things in the days before refrigeration. People worried that evil spirits might try to steal it, especially if it spilled. They tossed it over their left shoulders into the eyes of any salt-stealing demons.

WHY IT'S NONSENSE

Even if there *were* such things as demons, throwing salt in their eyes wouldn't stop them—at least not for long! In fact, salt occurs naturally in tears, which keep germs away and help prevent eye infections. (But don't actually *put* salt in your eyes—they have enough!)

Spooky Myth Busted

7 icky facts that will give you the creeps

1 The "**corpse flower**" grows up to 12 feet tall and smells like **rotting meat.**

2 A **coffin** was once designed to look like a **lobster.**

3 A man **sculpted a statue** of himself using his own **hair, teeth, and nails.**

4 In ancient Egypt, **mummies' brains** were removed through the **nose.**

5 Mike the **chicken** set a world record by living for **18 months** without a head, from 1945 to 1947.

6 **Phasmaphobia** is the **fear of ghosts.**

7 **Cat urine** can **glow** under **black light.**

FUNNY FILL-IN

Halloween Surprise!

Ask someone to give you words to fill in the blanks in this story without showing it to him or her. Then read it out loud for a laugh.

Halloween is the _____ holiday of the _____. This year I decided to dress as
(adjective ending in -est) _____ _(time period)_

_____. So I wore my _____ _____ on my _____ and a(n)
(movie character) _(adjective)_ _(type of clothing)_ _(body part)_

_____ on my _____. Then _____, my pet _____, and I
(noun) _(different body part)_ _(a relative's name)_ _(animal)_

_____ outside to go trick-or-treating. We expected to see at least _____ kids in the
(past-tense action verb) _(big number)_

street, _____ on every _____, and _____ in the _____.
(fruit, plural) _(part of a house)_ _(item found in the bathroom, plural)_ _(object in nature, plural)_

Instead, the streets were completely _____, and there were no kids for _____ miles around.
(adjective) _(number)_

Something very _____ was going on! As we started _____ toward home, I noticed
(adjective) _(action verb ending in -ing)_

lots of _____ in our driveway, and heard a(n) _____ noise coming from the
(type of transportation, plural) _(adjective)_

house. Suddenly I saw that the whole neighborhood was at my house to throw us a surprise _____
(holiday)

party. But before they saw us, we sneaked into the _____, put on our _____
(room in the house) _(adjective)_

masks, and jumped out of a(n) _____ yelling, "_____!" Everyone _____
(noun) _(exclamation)_ _(past-tense action verb)_

at least _____ feet in the air and then burst out _____. Guess the joke was on them!
(number) _(verb ending in -ing)_

FOODERSTITIONS

CAN YOU PREDICT YOUR FUTURE WITH THESE FOOD SUPERSTITIONS?

Will you ace your math test? Are you getting an iPod for your birthday? The secrets to your future may lie in your food. But be sure to study for that test no matter what—these activities are just for fun.

ASK A BANANA A QUESTION

Need an answer fast? Pick up a banana and ask it a yes-or-no question. Peel the banana, then make one slice near the end of it. If the lines in the center form a Y, the answer is yes. If not, the answer is no.

WISH UPON A SLICE OF CHEESE

Find out when your dreams will become reality. Make a wish. Then cut one slice off a block of Swiss cheese. Count the holes in your slice to find out how many weeks may pass before your wish comes true.

TWIST OF FATE

Want to know who your next friend will be? Twist an apple stem, reciting one letter of the alphabet with each turn. The letter you say when the stem breaks off could be the first initial of your new friend's name.

TELL YOUR FORTUNE WITH TEA LEAVES

FORTUNE TELLERS HAVE read tea leaves for hundreds of years. They believe that patterns you see in your tea leaves are symbols of what may happen in your future. Now discover what your tea could be telling you.

BREW A POT OF HOT TEA using loose tea leaves or leaves emptied from tea bags. Pour yourself a cup, then drink the tea or slowly pour out the liquid, keeping the leaves inside the cup.

WHAT PATTERN DO YOU SEE in your tea leaves? Use the chart below to find out what some common symbols mean. You may see other symbols, too. For more information about reading tea leaves, go to teausa.com.

TEA LEAF SYMBOLS

PATTERN	MEANING
CRESCENT MOON	GOOD LUCK
DOG	GOOD FRIEND
CAT	DISHONESTY
HOUSE	SECURITY
HEART	LOVE
KITE	A WISH THAT MAY COME TRUE

ASK FOR A PARENT'S HELP BEFORE USING A KNIFE OR BOILING WATER.

HAUNT YOUR HOUSE

You'll need these supplies for making almost everything shown here: scissors, paintbrushes, glue, heavy-duty stapler, and black duct tape.

TIP! WORK WITH AN ADULT TO CREATE THESE CREEPY CRAFTS.

1 SPLAT WITCH

YOU WILL NEED

RED OR ORANGE YARN • WITCH'S HAT • 2 PAIRS ADULT-SIZE KNEE SOCKS (STRIPED OR BLACK) • LOTS OF PLASTIC GROCERY BAGS FOR STUFFING • RED TAPE (OPTIONAL) • CARDBOARD RECTANGLE CUT 1 FOOT WIDE BY 2 FEET LONG • BLACK CAPE • OLD PAIR OF DARK-COLOR GLOVES • OLD SNEAKERS OR BOOTS • FISHING LINE • BROOM

WHAT TO DO

HEAD Cut yarn into foot-long pieces and tape them to the witch's hat to create hair.

ARMS AND LEGS Stuff both pairs of socks. (Hint: You can stripe solid-color socks with red tape.)

BODY Use the cardboard for the witch's body. Tape the arms and legs onto the cardboard, and then staple the hat and cape in place. Put on the stuffed gloves, then the shoes. Tape in place.

CRASH LANDING Ask an adult to mount the witch to a tree or wall with fishing line. Balance the broom in a tree limb or detach the broom from the pole and tape the broom end to the cardboard. To support the arms and legs, tie fishing line around them and string them to tree branches. Another option is to lay the witch facedown as if it has crashed into the ground.

2 GRISLY GRAVESTONES

YOU WILL NEED

• LARGE PIECES OF CARDBOARD
• GRAY AND WHITE CRAFT PAINTS
• WOODEN PAINT STIRRERS

WHAT TO DO

"CARVE" THE STONE Cut a gravestone shape out of cardboard.

PAINT IT Paint the cardboard gray. When dry, paint spooky messages with white paint.

MAKE A CEMETERY To place several gravestones in your yard, stick paint stirrers in the ground and prop the gravestones up against them. Tape onto the back to secure.

3 SCARY BATS

WHAT TO DO

BODY Roll a piece of paper into a tube and staple in place. Flatten one end and staple the front of the tube to the back. Cut an arch into that end to make a tail. Cut the other end to form ear shapes.

WINGS Cut identical wing shapes out of two pieces of paper. Staple both wings to the back of the tube.

EYES Use paint or reflective stickers to create eyes.

LET 'EM FLY Tape the bats to a wall or string them from a tree with fishing line.

4 MUMMY

WHAT TO DO

BODY Stuff the pants and shirt. Tuck the shirt inside the pants and pin in place.

WRAPPING Wind the sheet strips around the body until it's covered, tying knots to string the strips together.

HEAD Turn the milk jug upside down with the handle facing the back. Place a paint stirrer halfway into the jug. Push the other half into the stuffing at the neck. Wrap the jug.

HANDS AND FEET Sit the mummy in a chair, then place the pant legs inside the shoes and wrap the feet. Place the sleeves inside the stuffed gloves and wrap the hands.

EYES Cut eyes out of construction paper and glue to the head.

YOU WILL NEED

ADULT-SIZE OUTFIT OF OLD CLOTHES: JEANS, LONG-SLEEVE SHIRT, GLOVES, SNEAKERS • LOTS OF CRUMPLED NEWSPAPER FOR STUFFING • SAFETY PINS • 2 FULL-SIZE WHITE SHEETS CUT INTO LONG STRIPS • WOODEN PAINT STIRRER • GALLON-SIZE PLASTIC MILK JUG • BLACK CONSTRUCTION PAPER

I'LL BE BACK

I.M. GONE

YOU WILL NEED

STYROFOAM BALL ABOUT 6 INCHES IN DIAMETER (AVAILABLE IN CRAFT STORES) • RED CRAFT PAINT • LARGE PIECE OF CARDBOARD • 4 LARGE BLACK TRASH BAGS WITH DRAWSTRINGS • LOTS OF CRUMPLED NEWSPAPERS OR PLASTIC GROCERY BAGS FOR STUFFING • 16 RUBBER BANDS

5 GIANT SPIDER

WHAT TO DO

EYES Ask an adult to cut the Styrofoam ball in half. Paint each half red. Let dry.

RED MARKING ON BACK (optional) Cut a stripe shape (see spider in photo) out of cardboard and paint it red. Let dry.

LEGS Cut a trash bag lengthwise into four equal strips. Repeat with a second bag. Tape the long sides of the strips closed, but leave the tops open. Then turn the legs inside out. Stuff each leg halfway and fasten with a rubber band. Stuff the rest of the leg and tie the end with a rubber band.

HEAD Stuff a third garbage bag until it's half full and knot tightly.

BODY Stuff the fourth garbage bag until it's full. Use the bags' drawstrings on the body to tie the head and body together.

PUT IT TOGETHER Tape four legs to each side of the spider, and then tape on the eyes and red stripe as shown.

Just Joking

Owl

KNOCK, KNOCK

Who's there?
Who.
Who who?
Is there an owl in there?

ANOTHER LAME JOKE

Q How do you make a witch itch?

A Take away her w.

Q What did the **eyeballs** say to each other?

A Just between the two of us, something smells!

Q Why don't mummies go on vacation?

A They're afraid they might relax and unwind.

TONGUE TWISTER!

Say this fast three times:

Creepy crawly critters crunch.

Check out these 10 outrageous facts.

IT'S ILLEGAL TO SELL A **HAUNTED HOUSE** IN NEW YORK **WITHOUT TELLING** THE BUYER.

Abracadabra used to be written in a triangle shape to keep away evil spirits.

ABRACADABRA
ABRACADABR
ABRACADAB
ABRACADA
ABRACAD
ABRACA
ABRAC
ABRA
ABR
AB
A

No **words** in the dictionary rhyme with **"orange."**

Owls can't m**o**ve their eyeballs.

A **3,000-YEAR-OLD MUMMY** CAN STILL HAVE **FINGERPRINTS.**

Some people get **goosebumps** on their faces.

GHOST BATS are some of the only bats with **WHITE FUR.**

TARANTULAS CAN LIVE FOR UP TO **20** YEARS.

Your **skeleton** has about **300 BONES** when you are born, but only **206** when you grow up.

PUMPKINS ALSO COME IN **RED, GREEN, YELLOW, BLUE, TAN, & WHITE.**

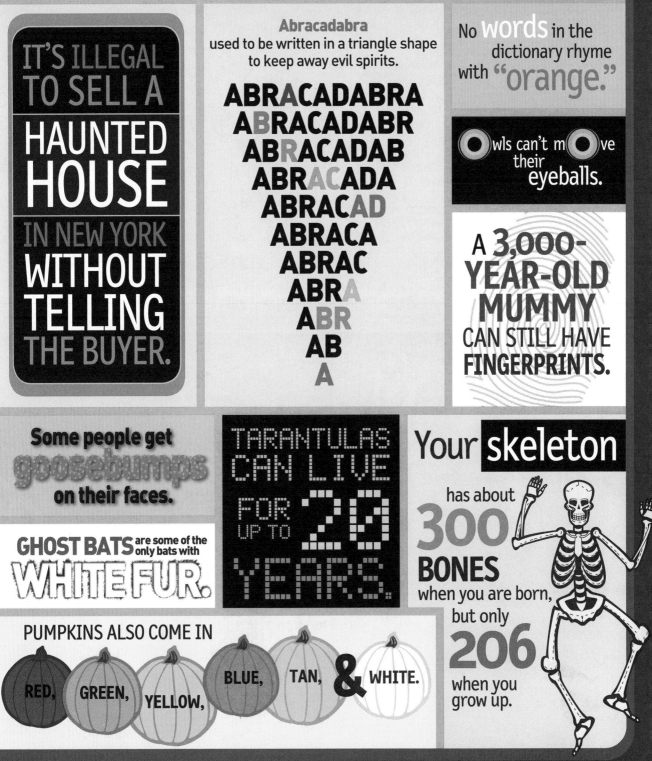

Costume Chaos

A group of friends spent the day at a fall festival (top). Examine each person closely, then match each person to the costume he or she wore to a Halloween party later (bottom). ANSWERS ON PAGE 78

We Gave It a Swirl

Use the clues below to figure out which animals appear in these swirled pictures. **ANSWERS ON PAGE 78**

1

2

HINT: This furry friend has orange and black spots—*purr*-fect for Halloween.

HINT: This animal's stripes help it stay camouflaged in a herd.

3

4

HINT: Hold your nose! This small creature can make a big stink.

5

HINT: These slinky stalkers live only in Asia.

HINT: This unusual amphibian is named for its tomato color.

Back Talk

Trick or doggy treat?

What do YOU think this dog is thinking? Fill in your own funny quote.

Spooky Myth Busted

SUPERSTITION

Walking under a ladder is bad luck.

WHERE IT CAME FROM

In ancient times, people believed that triangles were sacred. Walking through one (in this case, the triangle is formed by the ladder and the ground) could break the triangle's good powers and let evil things escape.

WHY IT'S NONSENSE

Triangles aren't sacred. They are just three connected points that aren't in a row. In fact, math experts such as professor Albert L. Vitter think of rectangular forms—such as doorways—as two triangles. (Picture a line from one corner of a doorway to its diagonal corner.) That means when you walk through a doorway, you're walking through two triangles. And so far, you're fine! (Still, don't walk under ladders—stuff could fall on your head!)

Photo Find

Halloween Hunt

It looks like this trick-or-treater got a lot more than candy for Halloween. Find and circle these:

3 lizards	dolphin
pumpkin	5 basketballs
scorpion	construction cone
7 letters	candy corn
pony	frog
13 gum balls	breath mint
4 vehicles	elephant
2 toy people	dinosaur

BONUS: How many bats do you see?

ANSWERS ON PAGE 78

61

SWEET TALK

Each cartoon illustrates the name of a popular candy. We filled in the first one for you. You fill in the rest. When you've got a craving for the answers, turn to page 78.

1. __Life Savers__
2. _____
3. _____
4. _____
5. _____
6. _____

TREAT TRIVIA

Match each fact with the candy it describes, then write the correct letter in the space provided.

ANSWERS ON PAGE 78

1. M & M's _____

2. Hershey's Kisses _____

3. Jolly Rancher_____

4. Baby Ruth _____

5. Whoppers _____

6. Twizzlers _____

7. Hershey's Bites _____

8. Butterfinger _____

ⓐ Comes in ropes, strings, nibs, and bites.

ⓑ The number of these mini-candies sold in the U.S. in one year could circle Earth twice.

ⓒ Customers voted to add blue ones in 1995.

ⓓ This candy's name comes from an expression sportscasters used to describe baseball players who dropped the ball.

ⓔ Probably named for the puckering sound made when each piece lands on a steel roller in the factory.

ⓕ Called "Giants" when they were first sold in 1939, they were renamed a decade later.

ⓖ According to legend, this candy was named for U.S. President Grover Cleveland's daughter Ruth.

ⓗ Named for its western heritage.

The Funnies

Funny Fill-In
Halloween Haunting

Ask someone to give you words to fill in the blanks in this story without showing it to him or her. Then read out loud for a laugh.

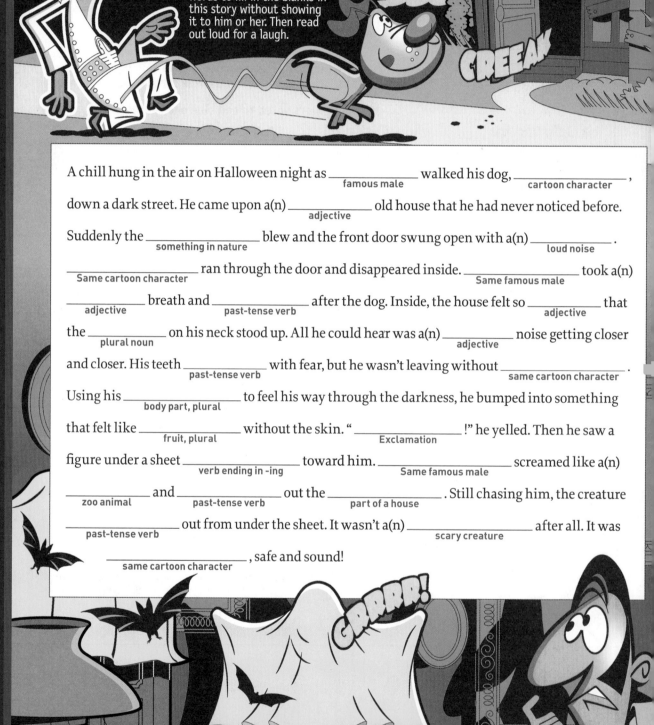

A chill hung in the air on Halloween night as _____ (famous male) walked his dog, _____ (cartoon character), down a dark street. He came upon a(n) _____ (adjective) old house that he had never noticed before. Suddenly the _____ (something in nature) blew and the front door swung open with a(n) _____ (loud noise). _____ (Same cartoon character) ran through the door and disappeared inside. _____ (Same famous male) took a(n) _____ (adjective) breath and _____ (past-tense verb) after the dog. Inside, the house felt so _____ (adjective) that the _____ (plural noun) on his neck stood up. All he could hear was a(n) _____ (adjective) noise getting closer and closer. His teeth _____ (past-tense verb) with fear, but he wasn't leaving without _____ (same cartoon character). Using his _____ (body part, plural) to feel his way through the darkness, he bumped into something that felt like _____ (fruit, plural) without the skin. "_____ (Exclamation)!" he yelled. Then he saw a figure under a sheet _____ (verb ending in -ing) toward him. _____ (Same famous male) screamed like a(n) _____ (zoo animal) and _____ (past-tense verb) out the _____ (part of a house). Still chasing him, the creature _____ (past-tense verb) out from under the sheet. It wasn't a(n) _____ (scary creature) after all. It was _____ (same cartoon character), safe and sound!

64

Just Joking

Spectacled caiman ▲

Q What does a skeleton order at a restaurant?

A Spareribs.

ANOTHER LAME JOKE

KNOCK,
KNOCK,

Who's there?
I won.
I won who?
I won to suck your blood!

Q Why was the **witch's broom** late to work?

A Because it overswept.

Q What kind of roads do ghosts haunt?

A Dead ends.

TONGUE TWISTER!

Say this fast three times:

Brenda's **bats** baked buttered **bread.**

What in the World?

Play interactive "What in the World?" and other games online. kids.nationalgeographic.com

TRICK OR TREAT?

These photographs show close-up and faraway views of things associated with Halloween. Unscramble the letters to identify what's in each picture.

ANSWERS ON PAGE 78

ULFL OMNO

_____

NYACD NRCO

_____

TBSA

_____

DCNAY LPEAP

_____

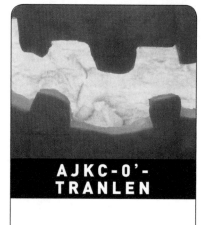

AJKC-O'-TRANLEN

_____

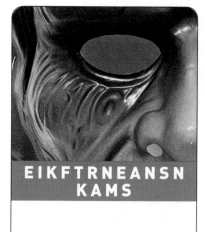

EIKFTRNEANSN KAMS

_____

DYGVAERAR

_____

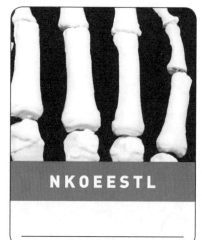

NKOEESTL

_____

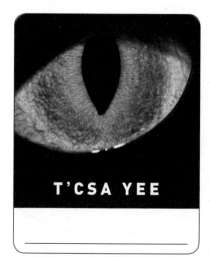

T'CSA YEE

_____

Pumpkin Stencils and Decals

HOW TO USE

1. Clean out your pumpkin.
2. Cut out a stencil.
3. Tape the stencil to your pumpkin.
4. Use a pushpin to poke holes around the pattern.
5. Take the paper pattern off the pumpkin.
6. With a parent's help, use child-safe carving tools to connect the holes and carve out the pattern.

Don't feel like carving? Use the flip side of these stencils as decals. Just glue them on to your pumpkin, or trace them on the pumpkin and paint inside the shapes.

STENCIL

The Cat's Meow

DECAL

A New Bat-itude!

STENCIL

DECAL

Perfect Pumpkin

STENCIL

DECAL

Awesome Arachnid!

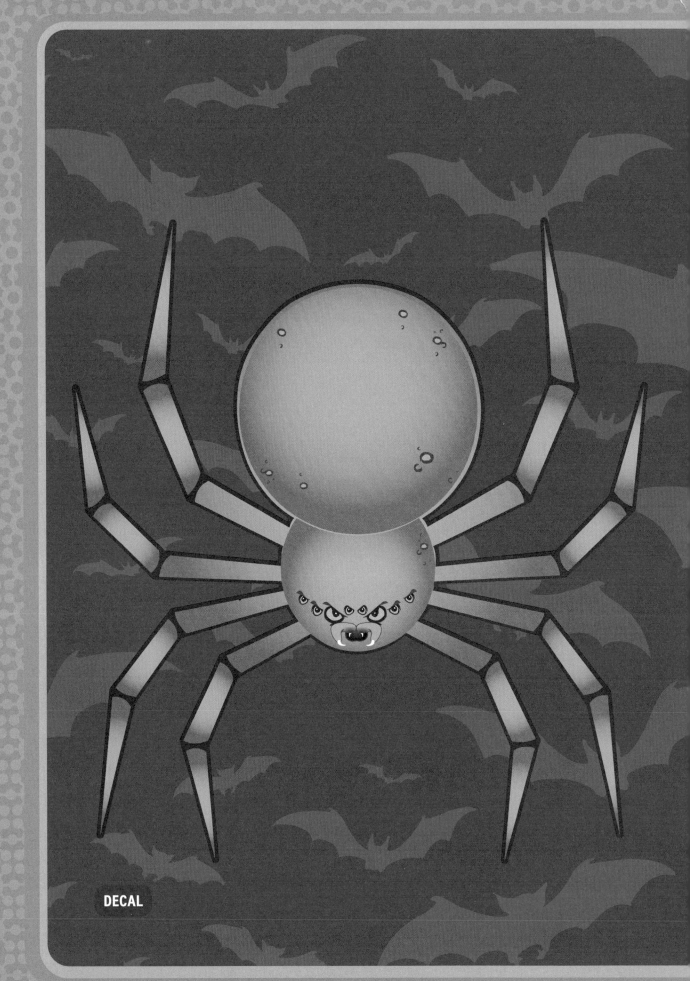

DECAL

Wicked
Witch

STENCIL

DECAL

Answers

Crazy Costumes, page 6

What in the World? Halloween Hues, page 7

TOP ROW: SNAKE, CARROT, LOG FIRE.
MIDDLE ROW: AUTUMN LEAF, BLACK PANTHER, APRICOTS.
BOTTOM ROW: DON'T WALK SIGN, POPPY FIELD, PENGUIN.

Monster Maze, page 9

Spellbound, page 10

1. BABOON, 2. EEL, 3. SNAKE, 4. DUCK, 5. OWL, 6. KITTEN,
7. OTTER, 8. PARROT, 9. CRICKETS, 10. SPIDER.

Hidden Halloween, page 12

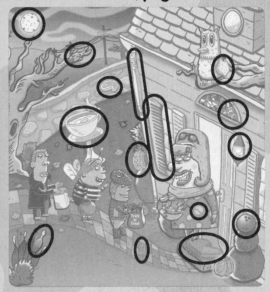

Find the Animals in Disguise, pages 22–23

1. G, 2. E, 3. H, 4. A, 5. B, 6. I, 7. J, 8. K, 9. F, 10. C, 11. D.

A *Boo*-tiful Halloween, page 24

(FROM LEFT TO RIGHT, TOP TO BOTTOM): ZOO, SHAMPOO, CANOE,
PERU, KANGAROO, SCREW, SHOE, BREW, GOO, GLUE.

Haunted Room, page 36

Costume Chaos, page 58

We Gave It a Swirl, page 59

1. CAT, 2. ZEBRA, 3. TIGER, 4. SKUNK, 5. TOMATO FROG.

What in the World?
Creepy Creatures, page 41

TOP ROW: SNAIL, SPIDER, BEETLE.
MIDDLE ROW: SEA SLUG, COCKROACH, CATERPILLAR.
BOTTOM ROW: WORMS, NEWT, MOLE.

Halloween Hunt, page 61

Crazy Cornucopia, page 43

Sweet Talk, page 62

1. LIFE SAVERS, 2. JUNIOR MINTS, 3. SNICKERS,
4. JOLLY RANCHER, 5. KIT KAT, 6. MILKY WAY.

Treat Trivia, page 63

1. C, 2. E, 3. H, 4. G, 5. F, 6. A, 7. B, 8. D.

Visual Tricks or Treats, page 45

THE SKELETONS ARE ALL THE SAME SIZE!

What in the World?
Trick or Treat?, page 66

TOP ROW: FULL MOON, CANDY CORN, BATS. **MIDDLE ROW:**
CANDY APPLE, JACK-O'-LANTERN, FRANKENSTEIN MASK.
BOTTOM ROW: GRAVEYARD, SKELETON, CAT'S EYE.

Published by the National Geographic Society

John M. Fahey, Jr., *Chairman of the Board and Chief Executive Officer*
Timothy T. Kelly, *President*
Declan Moore, *Executive Vice President, Publishing*
Melina Gerosa Bellows, *Executive Vice President, Chief Creative Officer, Books, Kids and Family*

Prepared by the Book Division

Nancy Laties Feresten, *Senior Vice President, Editor in Chief, Children's Books*
Jonathan Halling, *Design Director, Books and Children's Publishing*
Jennifer Emmett, *Editorial Director, Children's Books*
Carl Mehler, *Director of Maps*
R. Gary Colbert, *Production Director*
Jennifer A. Thornton, *Managing Editor*

Staff for This Book

Robin Terry, *Project Editor*
Eva Absher, *Art Director*
Lori Epstein, *Senior Illustrations Editor*
Ruthie Thompson, *Designer*
Kate Olesin, *Editorial Assistant*
Kathryn Robbins, *Design Production Assistant*
Hillary Moloney, *Illustrations Assistant*
Grace Hill, *Associate Managing Editor*
Sam Bardley, *Interim Associate Managing Editor*
Lewis R. Bassford, *Production Manager*
Susan Borke, *Legal and Business Affairs*

Based on the "Fun Stuff" department in NATIONAL GEOGRAPHIC KIDS **magazine**

Jill Yaworski, *Assistant Editor*
Nicole M. Lazarus, *Associate Art Director*
Kelley Miller, *Photo Editor*

Manufacturing and Quality Management

Christopher A. Liedel, *Chief Financial Officer*
Phillip L. Schlosser, *Senior Vice President*
Chris Brown, *Technical Director*
Rachel Faulise, *Manager*
Nicole Elliott, *Manager*
Robert L. Barr, *Manager*